Through St. Peter God says to all Christians: "You are . . . God's own people, that you may declare the wonderful deeds of Him who called you out of darkness into His marvelous light. Once you were no people but now you are God's people; once you had not received mercy but now you have received mercy." (1 Peter 2:9-10)

May this book undergird your faith and provide guidance for your Christian life. May you always rejoice in being one of God's own people and declare His wonderful deeds.

Yours in love,

Signed _Dad_

Date _May 22, 1977_

LIVING FOR CHRIST

LIVING FOR CHRIST

A Guide for the Newly Confirmed

by
William A. Kramer

Publishing House
St. Louis London

Concordia Publishing House, St. Louis, Missouri
Concordia Publishing House, Ltd., London, E. C. 1
Copyright © 1952, 1973 Concordia Publishing House
Library of Congress Catalog Card No. 72-96585
ISBN No. 0-570-03157-5

MANUFACTURED IN THE UNITED STATES OF AMERICA

CONTENTS

	Preface	9
I.	Your Promise to Christ	13
II.	Your Source of Strength	24
III.	Living for Christ at Home	38
IV.	Living for Christ in Your Work	51
V.	Living for Christ as a Church Member	64
VI.	Living for Christ Wherever You Are	78

PREFACE

As you thank God that you have reached the day of your confirmation, so your parents and friends thank Him likewise. They have seen you grow in faith and in the understanding of God's Word. They rejoiced when they saw the evidence of the Savior's love in your words and actions. To see young Christians confessing their faith and living according to it is a great joy. Even God and the angels in heaven rejoice over that. In spite of your sins and failings, you have often given God and His angels, as well as your fellow Christians, joy by the confession of your faith and your Christian life.

Your parents and friends, your pastor and Christian teachers, do not doubt your faith and sincerity. They know that you have confessed your faith and made your confirmation promise with the firm intention of keeping it, with the help of God. So you said, and so you meant it. Therefore you are safe and happy with your Lord and Savior Jesus Christ, through whom you have forgiveness of sins and eternal life. But others have made the same joyful confession and promise that you made, only to fall from grace in later years. The devil, who deceived them, will try to deceive you too. This concerns your parents, your pastor, your teachers, all your Christian friends, and you. It is important for you to know what to expect, and to know what to do in order to remain the same dear child of God that you are today.

This book is intended to help you in your Christian faith and life. Read it now. Reread it from time to time, and you will be reminded of many things that you will have to remember and do as a child of God. Read the prayers in the book; make your own prayers; read your Bible daily.

God bless you today and every day. God bless you for the promise which you made to Him of your own free will. God give you the strength to remain His own through the use of His Word and the Lord's Supper. God help you to live as a grateful child of His at home, in your work at school or at a job, in your worship and work as a church member, in your prayers, in your life and work everywhere. God wants to be close to you. Stay close to Him, and ask Him to keep you faithful, for Jesus' sake. Your parents and Christian friends are praying for you.

WILLIAM A. KRAMER

I. YOUR PROMISE TO CHRIST

The Most Important Promise You Ever Made

A person makes many promises during a lifetime. Some of these are more far-reaching than others, but every promise is important. "A promise is a promise," you have heard people say. Promises are to be kept, or they ought not to be made in the first place.

You have never given a more important promise than your confirmation vow. You know that, and therefore you did not make your vow lightly. In fact, you spent years in study and preparation in order to realize fully and exactly what it means. Then you made your vow, perhaps somewhat fearfully, but in the faith that God would enable you to keep it.

What You Promised

You promised that you would turn your back to the devil and serve only God. Your godparents had promised this for you at the time of your Baptism, when you were unable to speak for yourself. At your confirmation you repeated the promise in your own words with your own heart and lips.

You assured God that you believe in Him, the holy triune God, Father, Son, and Holy Spirit. In making your confession, you repeated the entire Apostles' Creed. Thus you promised to make the true God your own God, and not to follow the false gods of the world.

You told God that you believe the whole Bible, every word of it. You said also that you believe that the Lutheran Church teaches the Bible correctly and that therefore you wanted to be a member of the Lutheran Church.

You promised that you would remain true to God and His Word, even if you would have to suffer a martyr's death for your faith and confession.

Finally, you promised that you would continue to hear and learn the Word of God and that you, by God's power, would live according to it as He expects of all true Christians.

You Realized Your Own Weakness

You realized both the importance of your promise and the difficulty of keeping it, and so you did not say boldly: "Yes, Lord, I will keep my promise all right. You can depend on me." No, you remembered that thousands before you made the promise and that many of them failed. When asked whether you intend to keep your promise, you said, "I do so intend, with the help of God." What you meant was: "I cannot keep this solemn promise by my own power. I am much too weak to withstand the devil and his daily temptations, but God will help me keep my vow. I am weak, but He is strong, and He will help me, because He promised to do so." And so you made your vow cheerfully, trusting in God. That is the right way for a Christian to make the promises which God asks of him, confidently believing that God will enable him to keep them.

You Have Given Yourself Entirely to God

Your promise means that you have given yourself entirely to God. You will do well to remember that you do not belong one fourth nor one half to God, but altogether. Halfway surrender to God is never enough. Anything less than full surrender would mean that you were still not ready to give up the world with its sins and pleasures, but that you wanted to follow them and God at the same time. When Elijah met the Children of Israel and the prophets of Baal on Mount Carmel, Elijah, rebuking the Children of Israel, said: "How long will you sit on the fence? If the Lord is God, follow Him; but if Baal, then follow him" (1 Kings 18:21). You cannot take half and half, half God and half the world, but you have to choose one or the other. You chose God in faith.

A Story About an Indian Chief

You may have heard the story of the Indian chief who learned the lesson which also you will have to learn.

A pastor was preaching to the Indians on a northern reservation. An old Indian chief listened carefully to the message of Jesus and His love. He was deeply moved when the pastor said: "God so loved the world that He gave His only Son, that whoever believes in Him should not perish, but have eternal life" (John 3:16). Before long the chief slowly arose and came up with his tomahawk. As he laid it down, he said, "Indian chief give tomahawk to Jesus." Then he walked back to his place.

The pastor continued to preach about the love of Jesus and said that children of God serve Jesus with all their heart.

The chief listened attentively, but he was somewhat restless. Suddenly he got up, walked to the front, and laid down his blanket. As he did so, he said, "Indian chief give blanket to Jesus."

The pastor kept on speaking as though

he had not seen the Indian at all. Again he told of the goodness and love of Jesus and of the children of God who believe in Jesus and serve Him with all their heart. After some time the chief got up quietly and walked off into the woods. Soon he returned leading his pony. He marched to the front and said, "Indian chief give pony to Jesus." Then he walked back to where he had sat before and continued to listen.

The pastor went on as if nothing had happened and portrayed the love of Jesus more beautifully than ever. Then the old chief could stand it no longer. He walked up to the pastor, looked him squarely in the eyes, and said, "Indian chief give himself to Jesus." Then the pastor was satisfied. His Indian friend had learned that he could be a Christian only if he gave himself completely to Jesus and if he promised to serve Him with his whole heart.

Your Friends Are Happy About Your Promise

Your promise was worded differently, but it is the same which the Indian chief made. You told Jesus that He is your Lord and Savior and that you want to belong to Him forever. You were not forced to do it, yet you made your promise cheerfully in the sight of God and in the presence of your congregation. And by God's grace you expect to keep it. You came to a fork in the road where you had to choose between the wide road that leads to hell and the narrow road that leads to heaven, and you chose the road to heaven. You made a wise choice, and all Christians who know about it rejoice with you.

You Expect to Do Your Part

You have acknowledged to God that you are growing to Christian maturity and that with

His help and guidance you will live and act like a Christian grownup. You have told God that you appreciate His blessings, and you have promised that you will take on the responsibilities that go with these blessings. You have confessed that you are saved to serve God and that you are going to be more than an ornament in God's kingdom. You want to be a faithful worker, who will do his part and pull his part of the load. It is a great and glorious and far-reaching promise that you have made, and if you remember it and live by it, you will be a useful Christian worker and a good example to all who know you.

God Will Help You Keep Your Promise

You know perfectly well that you made a promise which will be hard to keep. It is not easy to live a morally upright life and to fight sin when so many people around you willingly surrender to sin. You know very well that the devil can make sin look innocent and pleasant to you, and yet you said: "I will fight the devil, with the help of God."

You are now right with God, and you have promised to stay right, to hear His Word, to pray, to live the way God wants you to live. You have promised this because you have experienced God's grace in the forgiveness of sins, and you know that nothing is so important as God's grace and forgiveness and eternal life.

Your confirmation promise will be a blessing to you as long as you keep it. It will haunt you and make you miserable when you break it, for your own conscience will condemn you. Your promise was a right promise, which you ought to keep. It is a promise which of your own free will you said you wanted to keep. And, best of all, God will help you keep your promise to your dying day if you do not brush His help thanklessly aside. Even your Savior Jesus Christ is praying for you as for all Christians: "Holy Father, keep them in Your name, which You gave Me." (John 17:11)

Prayer

Dear Father in heaven, I trust in Your grace and mercy. You know my sins and weaknesses, but You also know that I love You. Strengthen my faith, and help me to love You more and to serve You better. If I should ever forget You, do not forget me, but bring me back again and assure me of Your love and care. Bless my parents, pastors, teachers, godparents, and members of my confirmation class, and keep us ever faithful; in Jesus' name. Amen.

II. YOUR SOURCE OF STRENGTH

The Devil Will Tempt You

You will need a strong undergirding of faith to keep the vow which you have made to your Savior, because you will be in daily battle with Satan, who hates you and all Christians. Though you overcome him one day, he will be back the next with new temptations. He will come in pleasant forms, and at times he will be hard to recognize as the devil. You remember how he came to Jesus in the desert when Jesus was hungry. "You are hungry," he said, "when there is no need to be hungry. It isn't right that You should be hungry. Make bread out of these stones." You recall how piously Satan talked when he tried to induce

Jesus to jump from the high point of the Temple. This is the idea he tried to get across to Jesus: "Don't worry. You know that Your Father has mighty angels at Your service. They will protect You. And see how You can impress the people by leaping from the pinnacle of the Temple without being hurt." You know finally how he tempted Jesus with the riches of the world to get Jesus to worship the vilest character of all, the devil himself.

So the devil will tempt you. He may tempt you through the words and actions of your friends, the sinful pleasures of the world, or the lust and evil thoughts that arise in your own heart. He will try to make you doubt the truth of God's Word as he made Eve doubt when he asked, "Did God really say that?" He will try to fill your heart with hate, pride, greed, and lying and all the other sins against God's Commandments. He will especially try to make you think that you can get along without God. The thought of all this would be enough to frighten you if it were not for God's gracious promise to be with you and to strengthen you.

God's Strength Is Your Strength

When the devil tempts you, remember that God is right there too. God's strength will be your strength. Stay in touch with God through the means of communication which He has provided. He wants to speak to you in His Word — listen. He offers you the Lord's Supper for the forgiveness of sins and the strengthening of your faith — receive it. He offers to hear your prayers — speak to Him. That's how you can stay in touch with God in good and in bad times, when things run smoothly and when you are tempted.

You cannot, of course, save yourself, regardless of what you do or regardless of how much you pray. Jesus saved you wholly and fully when He suffered and died for you. You cannot come to faith by yourself. Faith comes from God the Holy Spirit. You cannot live a holy Christian life by your own power. The power to do this comes from God. God has done everything, and it is just this fact which should make God's power and love so real and so important to you.

The Means of Grace

God always gets in touch with you first. He communicates with you in three ways. He made you His child in your Baptism, when He gave you faith and the forgiveness of sins. Now that you are fairly growing up, God's grace comes to you in His Word and in the Lord's Supper. God's Word, Holy Baptism, and the Lord's Supper are called the means of grace, because through them God pours His grace into our lives. The means of grace are the only ways which God uses to speak to you. So you must use these to receive God's message and God's blessings.

If you were to stop reading and hearing God's Word, and if you were to refuse the Lord's Supper, you would shut God's grace out of your life. Pray God that may never happen.

Use the Means of Grace Faithfully

As a Christian you must always remember how you became a believer in the first place and how you continue to be a believer. You were brought to faith by Holy Baptism. As you grew up, you learned God's Word, and by means of that Word you grew in faith and were able to live a Christian life. Now that you are confirmed, the Lord's Supper is an additional means of strengthening your faith and Christian life. While the Word and the sacraments are the only means for nurturing your Christian faith and life, they are sure and powerful means.

You know what would happen if you failed to eat for several weeks. After only a few days you would present a pitiful sight. You would be pale and weak, your cheeks would sink in, and you would lose all joy of life and all ambition. Before long you would have to stay in bed, and within a few weeks at most you would be dead. Man cannot live without food, for that is the way God made man. Exactly the same thing happens spiritually to people who stop reading and hearing God's Word and going to the Lord's Supper. Their faith begins to wither and die; their conscience becomes uncertain, and they are not sure anymore what is right and what is wrong. Gradually it becomes much easier for them to sin: to curse and swear, to gamble, to be disobedient to parents and government, to lie, steal, think unclean thoughts and do unclean deeds, to talk evil of their neighbors, and to do all the other things that God forbids. No one can escape this gradual spiritual death if he does not use the power which God makes available to Him in His Word and in the Lord's Supper. Thousands have tried and failed. You will fail if you neglect the means of grace. That is why God pleads with you to hear His Word, to sanctify the holy day, and to come to the Lord's Supper often. He wants you to have the necessary strength of faith. He wants to feed you with His life-giving Word. If Jesus loved you enough to suffer and die for you on the cross, and if He knows what is best for you and offers it, can you refuse to take it and to receive it thankfully?

God's Word can be a great power for you. It can strengthen your faith, keep you from ruining your life by sin, give you hope, courage, and confidence, and greater joys than you can find anywhere else. In sorrow it can comfort you, in weakness strengthen you, in temptation uphold you. It can give you the strength to go forward when others go backward, to do right when others do wrong, to pray when others scoff, to keep you faithful when your sinful heart tempts you to forsake God. There is nothing that God cannot do for you if you will let Him. His Word can guide you safely from day to day. "Blessed are they that hear the Word of God and keep it." (Luke 11:28)

The Power of Prayer

God speaks to the Christian, but the Christian also speaks to God in prayer. Prayer is a wonderful privilege. It is talking to God.

Talking to God in prayer is even easier than talking to your friends, for God is closer to you than anyone else. To talk to your friends, they must be near you, or within shouting distance, or at the end of a telephone line. You can talk to God anywhere, at any time. You can be much more intimate with Him than even with your parents or dearest friend. He understands you and your needs much better than they do. You can tell Him your joys and sorrows, your sins and worries, and all your needs. There is not a place where God is not with you, not a moment when He is not ready to help. So you can pray at any time for big things and little things, knowing that God will do what is best. There is unlimited strength in prayer. Martin Luther was a great man partly because he prayed so much. You know what power Abraham's prayers had, and David's, and the prayers of all Christians. "If you abide in Me, and My words abide in you, ask whatever you will, and it shall be done for you" (John 15:7). That is Jesus' promise. Prayer is a great source of strength for every Christian. It can make you strong.

Some Suggestions for Prayer

As a Christian you have long ago learned to pray, yet you might appreciate a few simple suggestions for your prayers: You can pray anywhere when the need arises, but you will often want to seek a quiet place for your prayers. You should spend some time each day in quiet prayer when no one else is near you and when there will be no distractions.

Speak to God in simple words as you would talk to an intimate friend. Tell Him about your sins, your worries, your weakness, but also about your joys. Acknowledge your unworthiness and God's grace. Ask for forgiveness. If there are special sins that trouble you, ask special forgiveness for them. Promise God that with His help you will do better in the future. Do not forget to thank God for all the good things in your life. Gratitude for God's goodness is the first mark of the Christian. Remember that if Jesus had not died for you, you would not even have the right to pray.

Pray for others, for your parents, brothers, sisters, relatives, friends, your pastor and teachers, for a troubled world, for unbelievers who will not accept Jesus as their Savior, even for your enemies if you have any, for all who need God's help and guidance in any way. Unselfish interest in the welfare of others is also a mark of the Christian.

Believe with all your heart that God will hear your prayer. He will do it every time if you pray in faith, for that is what He has promised.

Be ready to accept God's answer to your prayer even if it is not the answer that you expected. God has promised you everything that you need for your salvation. He has not promised you all earthly goods that you might want, but only what you need. Your ideas of what you need sometimes differ from God's. But you can always be sure that God is wiser than you. Ask God for anything that it is right to have, but never say, "Give it to me," as though God had to do so. Say, "If it is Your will, Lord, give it to me." Jesus in Gethsemane is your example for such prayer. Remember that He taught us to pray the Third Petition in the Lord's Prayer: "Thy will be done." It is God's will that all our spiritual and earthly needs should be supplied. We are to ask for them, and then leave everything to His will. He will always do what is right.

You Will Be Victorious

If you accept God's promise of salvation through Jesus Christ, and if you pray according to God's will, God's power will work in you. He will be your constant source of strength, and your faith and Christian life will be a joy to behold. Then you will not ask: "How often do I have to go to church? How often do I have to go to the Lord's Supper? How often do I have to pray?" Rather, you will realize that hearing and reading God's Word is a great privilege, for by it the strength of God flows into you. And so you will read God's Word, take part in your family devotions, and go to church and Bible class gladly. You will have a regular time for prayer, and you will pray often between the regular times. That will make your faith a strong faith, your religion a live and active religion, and you a strong Christian. And you will find it possible to keep your confirmation vow, with the help of God. You will find joy in serving God and your fellowmen and in doing all the things that you promised at your confirmation.

Nothing but the means of grace and prayer will keep you strong. But they will do so safely and surely. You will be victorious in your fight against the devil, because you will have God on your side. "If God is for us, who can be against us?" (Rom. 8:31)

Prayer

Lord God, Holy Spirit, give me the power of faith and the Christian life which only You can give. Give me joy in hearing You speak to me and help me to grow in grace through Your Word. Make Your strength my strength. Forgive all my sins and help me overcome temptation. Make me diligent and confident in prayer and keep me on the way of life; through Jesus Christ, my Lord and Savior. Amen.

III. LIVING FOR CHRIST AT HOME

Be Your Best at Home

It is likely that you will continue to live in your present home for some years to come. You will live with parents and with brothers and sisters; and, if anywhere, you should live as a Christian at home.

It is not right, as is so often the case, that people are the most unpleasant at home. We can go out and be happy and cheerful in the company of our friends, but when we get home, we may be grouchy and unpleasant. There is an explanation for such behavior. We are home so much more of the time, and we know the members of our own families so much more intimately than other people that we know all their weaknesses. In the case of people whom we meet less frequently, who act their best away from home just as we do, we are likely to see only the better qualities. As a result we misjudge values. We overlook the good qualities of our parents and brothers and sisters, and we overlook the faults of others with whom we are less well acquainted. Then when minor irritations arise at home, we become disagreeable and perhaps even unbearable. It is not necessary to tell you that this is all wrong. While love should rule us everywhere, it should direct our behavior especially in our family relationships. Try to be your best at home.

Remember the Debt You Owe Your Parents

You are to be closer to God than to anybody else. "You shall have no other gods."

That is the First Commandment. But of all the people on earth, until you get married yourself, your parents are to be the nearest and dearest to you. Never forget the debt you owe them. If it were not for them, you would not be here in the first place. If they had not taken care of you when you were a baby, you could not have lived long. They worked for you, lost sleep over you, fed you, kept you clean, and did everything for you for years, before you were able to take care of yourself even in part. They are supporting you now, except for minor earnings that you may have. Thousands of days of work, thousands of prayers, thousands of cares and worries, thousands of dollars, and great love have gone into your care and training. You can never repay that debt. But remembering the debt should make you thankful. Shouldn't it encourage you to love your parents, to obey them, to serve them cheerfully, and to ask their advice on important problems? They can help you, and they are seeking your best interests. Remember that.

Obey Your Parents

At the same time remember your duty to obey your parents. "Honor your father and mother, that it may be well with you and that you may live long on the earth" (Eph. 6:2-3). That is the Fourth Commandment. God even gives a special promise to obedient children. He does this to make obedience attractive and pleasant for them. You have learned enough from the Bible to know that He keeps this promise to obedient children and that He punishes the disobedient. Cain, Eli's sons, and Absalom show clearly enough that disobedient children destroy their chance for success and happiness. Solomon, Ruth, Timothy, and others show how God blesses the obedient. And if you carefully look around among the children and people whom you know, you will find examples of both kinds. "Children, obey your parents in everything, for this pleases the Lord." (Col. 3:20)

You Will Need Your Parents as You Grow Up

Though you will likely spend a good many more years in your present home, it is just as true that you will gradually grow away from your present home into one of your own. That is natural and desirable. Not that your love and care for the members of your family will grow less, but you will be less at home and more away. The time will come when you will go to work, perhaps away from home, and even your school may take more time than in the past. You may attend school far from home. Eventually you will want to marry, if it is God's will, and establish a home of your own. Then you will come to your present home only to visit. That is God's way, and it is a good way. It is all part of growing up. Your parents will want you to grow up, and they will help you in every way they can if you will be decent and Christian about it. But as you grow up, if you are wise, you will still seek your parents' advice and guidance. You will need it.

Advice on Growing Up

In order to make your growing-up process smooth and satisfactory and God-pleasing, you will have to grow up God's way.

1. As Christians both you and your parents will always keep in mind that everything is to be done to God's glory and according to God's will. Our will does not count unless it agrees with God's will. You will sometimes find it hard to submit to God's will, because you are a great imitator. You will want to do what others do — your friends, schoolmates, and neighbors. They will not always do what is right. Because you are a sinner, you will sometimes forget what God wants, and you will want what you want. If you use God's Word and the Sacrament and pray diligently, there will be less danger for you, because you will come back on the right track. But you will always have to be watchful. We Christians can get too sure of ourselves, and that is dangerous. Remember what happened to Peter when he forgot to watch and pray. So make up your mind anew every day that with God's help you will always want what God wants. You will be surprised what that will do for the happiness of your entire life. "Whatever you do, do all to the glory of God." (1 Cor. 10:31)

2. You will have to know how to deal with sins and failings. Your parents, your brothers, and you are all sinners. Sin brings unhappiness and other difficulties into your home. It brought unhappiness into the homes of Adam and Eve, of Jacob, and of every other believer at times. Overlook the sins and failings of others in your family as you expect them to overlook yours. Ask for forgiveness when you have offended them, and be ready to forgive when you have been wronged. Right attitudes of love, kindness, forbearance, and forgiveness are absolutely necessary. Then your actions will be right, and your homelife happy. "Forgive us our sins as we have forgiven those who sin against us." (Matt. 6:12)

3. Be thankful. Every real Christian is a thankful person. He is thankful for God's grace and mercy in Jesus Christ. If you are truly thankful for that, you will be thankful to those about you, your parents and others. Thankfulness is one of the first requirements for happiness; selfishness and ingratitude will ruin your chance for happiness. Thank your parents in words and deeds for all that they have done. Do not be ashamed to tell them how much you love them and how grateful you are to them. "Be thankful." (Col. 3:15)

4. Contribute to the upkeep of your home if you earn wages. You need a good home, and you want a good home, but remember that also you are responsible for its success and upkeep. No matter how much you give back in money or service, you can never repay your parents for what they have done. Do not wait until your parents ask you to pay board or to turn over part of your earnings. As soon as you earn, talk matters over with them, and ask them what they think is fair. Tell them that you are now in a position to help along and that you want to pay for part of the family maintenance, that you want to pay for your clothes or for part of your schooling. Be generous, and do not withhold as much as you can withhold, but give as much as you can give. That will make for God's blessing and for happiness. But whether you have money to contribute to the upkeep of the home or not, help with the work at home. "In love serve one another." (Gal. 5:13)

5. Spend as much time with members of your family as possible. Your home is not in the streets, in the shows or taverns, or in the many other places where Christians are tempted to be led astray. Certainly, you will need recreation away from home, but let it be the kind of recreation of which God approves. Sometimes you will go out with your parents, sometimes you will go with your friends, and sometimes alone, but your main place is at home, even after you have started to grow up. Teen-agers are sometimes reluctant to go out with their parents or to join in their activities. But remember that joint family activities are necessary for building homes in which every member appreciates the blessings of the home, in which he appreciates his parents and brothers and sisters, in which he realizes his responsibilities and becomes ready to give his services for the general good. You may have heard the slogan "Families that pray together stay together." It is also partly true that families that play together stay together. Join in the activities of your family, and your life will be the better for it. Music, games, and hobbies are invaluable for this purpose.

6. Always remember that you are looking forward to the day when you will establish your own home and family. The quality of a home depends on the quality of the people that make up the home. Be sure you develop the qualities that will make you a substantial member of your future home and family. Live God's way, and obey His laws of reverence, obedience, decency, honesty, and love. Decency and chastity are especially important for you if you are to become a worthy husband or wife someday. Many young people have thrown aside their obedience to God and parents, as well as their decency, for a brief moment of pleasure, only to be sorry ever afterwards. The health and happiness of an entire life can be ruined by giving way to the sins against the Sixth Commandment. Joseph is an example for young people of all times. Pray to God for strength as he did. Keep away from places where you know that you will be tempted, and build a chaste and decent life that will be a joy to God and His angels, to yourself, to your parents, and to Christians everywhere. "Create a pure heart in me, O God." (Ps. 51:10)

Prayer

Dear Savior Jesus Christ, thank You for loving me. Help me to love You and the members of my family as You love me. At home and everywhere help me to be happy and useful. Forgive my sins and make me willing to forgive as You forgive. When I grieve my parents, give me the decency to seek their forgiveness. In due time bring me to my eternal home above. Amen.

IV. LIVING FOR CHRIST IN YOUR WORK

Work Is One of God's Blessings

You will probably have four years of high school ahead of you and, if you are fortunate, some years of college as well. What does that mean to you? Whether you go on to school for a number of years, or whether you soon get a job, you are going to work in a real sense.

It is important to realize that work is a great blessing. To hear some people talk, it does not seem to be. They complain if they have to work hard or even if minor difficulties occur in their work. Such people do not know what life is all about. As a Christian you cannot think as they do. Man worked even before the Fall, for God put him into the Garden of Eden "to till it and keep it." Even if there were no sin, we would still have to work. Since man's fall into sin, work has become more difficult. You recall what God told Adam after the Fall: "Cursed is the ground because of you; in toil shall you eat of it all the days of your life. . . . In the sweat of your face you shall eat bread" (Gen. 3:17-19). In spite of the fact that work is sometimes unpleasant, it is a blessing. It helps us to make a living. Work keeps our minds and hands busy, and thus it often keeps us out of sin. It provides us with an opportunity to serve God by serving our fellow human beings. We can make their lives easier and happier through the crops we raise, the products we manufacture, and through the services which are part of today's world. And the money we get for our work enables us to give for the needs of God's work on earth.

Make the Most of Your School

Your schooling is work. It is part of life itself and a preparation for life and for further useful work. The more diligently you work in school, the better you will be prepared for the profession or occupation you will choose, and the more satisfactory and useful your life will be. School is a preparation for service. Looking at it in that light, you will enjoy and appreciate your school more, you will study and work harder, and you will profit more. Many students are unhappy in school and make poor grades because they do not look at school as a preparation for useful service and a happy life. Make the most of your school years. If you are fortunate enough to attend a Christian high school or college, be doubly grateful for your opportunities.

Faithful Work Brings Satisfactions

Dislike of work is really quite unnatural. Work is essential for everybody, even for the rich who do not need to work for a living. They need to work to do good to their fellowmen. Work brings great and lasting satisfactions to people who know what life is all about. They have the satisfaction of being useful and of doing God's will. They are grateful for the privilege of making their own living, grateful to God that they are not sick or crippled and dependent for their living on the good will of others. They are grateful that they can earn money with which they can do good, which they can use for the building of God's kingdom and for helping people who are in need.

One of the greatest satisfactions in your work will come to you when you do your work well enough to be promoted to greater service and greater responsibilities. Promotion to a better position is also one of God's blessings on faithful work.

Choose Useful Work

The satisfactions of work come to people who are engaged in a useful occupation. Earning money for the support of a family, or being a good mother and housewife, brings great satisfactions because of its usefulness. The same would not be true if you chose work by which others are damaged and exploited. You will readily understand that a gambler or racketeer, or the person engaged in any occupation that harms others, cannot get the satisfaction of service out of his work. In preparing for a job and in choosing your job be careful to look toward one that not only provides a living for you, but also enables you to serve God and benefit your fellowman. Study hard, develop the ability to think, make up your mind that you will serve God first, keep physically fit, profit from past mistakes, and you will have little trouble finding work which you can do and enjoy and in which you can serve God and your fellowmen.

Choosing Your Lifework

You may be concerned about the kind of occupation that you will finally choose as your lifework. You may wonder whether you will really find something that you can do well and that you will like to do. You have little to worry about here. There are hundreds of different jobs and many different kinds of work. There may be certain work which you simply could not like and in which you could not be happy. You will not want to choose that.

However, most people can get used to many different kinds of work.

As you go to school, or even after you have taken a job, you can read about various occupations, and you can get advice and guidance from your school and others. There are tests which show for which kinds of work you are especially fitted. Your high school can advise you regarding these. You can try out different kinds of work on a part-time basis during your high school years. But more important than all these are your determination to work and to make yourself useful in some honorable occupation that will enable you to make an honest living for yourself and for your future family. Your job will have much to do with the good which you will be able to do. Study and work hard, and ask God to guide you.

As a boy, Abraham Lincoln had few

books. He had to do his reading and studying by the light of the fireplace. Make the most of your modern schools, books, and conveniences.

You May Want to Become a Church Worker

As you think about a lifework, do not forget that the church needs pastors, teachers, professors, deaconesses, and workers in other positions. It is every Christian's duty to see that these positions are filled. That duty goes farther than to see that the salaries of church workers are paid. Each individual Christian must consider whether he should not personally serve. You would be shocked if you were suddenly told that all young people had refused to become church workers and that the church's colleges and seminaries would therefore be closed. You would think forty years ahead, and you would see the church dying for lack of workers. But did it ever occur to you that no boy or girl has a greater duty to become a pastor or teacher or deaconess or other full-time church worker than you have? Why should your friend or neighbor, or the boy or girl in another congregation, feel more compelled to prepare for full-time service in the church than you? Their responsibilities are no greater than yours. Think it over, and if you are qualified, ask God what your duty and opportunity are in the matter. He will guide you. Obviously, not all boys and girls can or should go into the full-time service of the church, but you may be one of those who should. That is why you should think and pray over the matter.

Work Is an Adventure

Besides being a great blessing of God, work is an adventure that should appeal to every healthy boy and girl. You do not want to rust out like the idle watch or automobile, but you want to go out and be active and do things that are worthwhile. You will want to pay the price of success. This price comes high, but it is worth it. The price you will have to pay is self-discipline, continued effort, punctuality, study, courage, industry, honesty, dependability, open-mindedness, willingness to perform unpleasant tasks, profiting from mistakes, and faithful service. You will have to be willing to start early in life to train for your job. You will have to grow on the job, to try to please your employer and your fellow workers, but mainly to do what is right. Successful work is largely a matter of right attitudes, love for work in general, love for your particular work, confidence that you can do the job, willingness to work hard, and joy in serving God. These attitudes will make you the kind of worker that employers want, also the kind of worker that is eventually able to go into business for himself, because he has learned the fundamentals of work and of getting along with others.

Be the Kind of Worker God Wants

You will want to be the kind of worker God wants. If you have never checked the Bible to see what God says about work, you will have a surprise coming. You have already seen how God instituted work in the Garden of Eden. Listen to this:

Eccl. 9:10: "Whatever your hand finds to do, do it with your might."

Eph. 4:28: "Let the thief no longer steal, but rather let him labor, doing honest work with his hands, so that he may be able to give to those in need."

Prov. 13:4: "The soul of the sluggard

craves, and gets nothing, while the soul of the diligent is richly supplied."

Prov. 24:30-31: "I passed by the field of a sluggard, by the vineyard of a man without sense; and lo, it was all overgrown with thorns; the ground was covered with nettles, and its stone wall was broken down."

Prov. 13:11: "Wealth hastily gotten will dwindle, but he who gathers little by little will increase it."

2 Thess. 3:10: "If anyone will not work, let him not eat."

These are only a few of the many words of Scripture which show that work is honorable, that God expects us to work, and that He blesses honest work, whatever it may be. If you become a good worker, you will be on God's side, and His blessings will attend you, and you will find hundreds of ways of making yourself useful.

Prayer

Gracious God, thank You for the forgiveness of my sins and for the privilege of work. Help me to find useful work in which I can serve You and my fellowmen. Guide me in using my earnings wisely for my own good, for the work of the church, and also to share them with the needy. And, Lord, if You should want me to become a full-time church worker, help my parents and me to see this as Your will. Bless me with an eagerness to serve You and the people around me; for the sake of Your great love for me. Amen.

V. LIVING FOR CHRIST AS A CHURCH MEMBER

God Expects You to Be a Faithful Church Member

God expects you to be a faithful church member, for your own good. "He who is of God hears the words of God" (John 8:47). "Let the Word of Christ dwell in you richly" (Col. 3:16). "Blessed are those who hear the Word of God and keep it" (Luke 11:28). These are all words of God that you have learned from memory. Live by them and you will be happy.

As a Member of the Church You Have Responsibilities

Through Holy Baptism you became a member of the church. God gave you faith, because He wants you to be a member of His kingdom here on earth and He wants you in heaven. You are a baptized member and, since your confirmation, also a communicant member of the church. Your church is concerned about your spiritual welfare. When you were baptized and also when you were confirmed, the whole congregation prayed for you. Your parents, your pastor, and your teachers have prayed for you. Your congregation has helped your parents in giving you a Christian education, in Sunday school, perhaps in a Christian day school, and in confirmation your congregation said in effect that now you are old enough to take on more responsibility. You are growing into a mature

Christian who knows Christian teachings, who can examine his (or her) own faith and life, who can receive the Lord's Supper, and who can assume much greater responsibility than heretofore. You are in the position of the 12-year-old Jesus, who went to the temple at Jerusalem for the first time because He had reached the age when He was beginning to be considered grown-up and responsible for many more things than formerly. How will you carry out your responsibility?

If Your Heart Is Right, You Will Go to Church

God made you a member of the communion of saints (the company of believers). He invites and expects you to go to church. If in spite of God's loving invitation you fail to respond, you will have to take the consequences of your actions. You will always remember, too, that God is not interested in mere outward church membership. Ananias and Sapphira were members of the church in good standing until God revealed their hypocrisy and called them to judgment. Their hearts were not right. God wants your heart, and if you give Him your heart, then your active church membership and your partaking of Holy Communion will follow naturally. Your love for God's Word and your worship will show that your heart is right with God.

Come to Worship

One of the important reasons for belonging to church and for going to church is worship. God praised the first Christians because "they devoted themselves to the apostles' teaching and fellowship, to the breaking of bread and the prayers" (Acts 2:42). You, too, will want to confess your faith with your fellow

Christians and worship with them because that is one of the blessings which God intends for you. You will want to do it also because after this life you want to meet your parents, friends, relatives, Abraham, Moses, St. Paul, Martin Luther, and all the rest who have gone to heaven before you.

One of the great blessings of church membership is found in uniting in worship with the congregation. In your worship you show that you honor and respect God. You show your great love and admiration for Him. You show also that you share the saving faith with fellow Christians and rejoice with them in being God's people.

Helps in Worship

To get the greatest benefit from your worship in church, there are a number of points which you ought to keep in mind:

1. Come to church as a humble sinner. Pride cannot stand in God's presence. Come to rid yourself of the burden of your sin; come to strengthen your faith. Expect confidently that God will do these things for you.

2. Remember that churchgoing is not only a duty, but a great privilege as well. That will bring joy and gratitude into your heart. Without gratitude you cannot worship. Churchgoing should be a grateful and joyful experience. Jesus Christ has redeemed you, a poor, miserable sinner, and therefore you can worship joyfully.

3. Attend church regularly. There should be no question about your attending church on Sunday unless some compelling reason prevents you. While churchgoing should not be only a habit, it must certainly be also a habit, or you will neglect it.

4. Get ready for Sunday on Saturday.

Many people neglect church attendance because they stay out too late on Saturday night and on Sunday morning they are tired and irritable. Sunday worship is always more important than any Saturday night event, important as it may seem.

5. When you get to church, take your seat and say a silent prayer. In this prayer you can talk anything over with God, but ask Him especially to bless your worship and to cheer and comfort you spiritually. Ask God to be gracious to you for Jesus' sake, and thank Him for His blessings. If you have time, read the hymns that are posted to get the spirit of the service.

6. Be sure you leave worries and ill will at home. You are in the presence of God, who has only blessings for you, and you have no cause for worry or ill will toward your neighbor.

7. Expect great blessings to come to you.

Come in the spirit of Jacob, who said as he wrestled with the Angel of God: "I will not let You go, unless You bless me" (Gen. 32:26). God has promised to bless you. Expect Him to do it.

8. Apply the sermon to yourself. It is easy to think while listening to a sermon: "This is for John"; "My parents ought to remember that"; "I guess the pastor meant Mary with that"; and so on. But such thinking is all wrong. God's Word is for everyone, and as far as you are concerned, it is for you. Let the others in church apply it to themselves as you apply it to yourself.

9. Praise God with all your heart. Remember that you are in the presence of God. It should be a glorious feeling to know that God is so near that He speaks to you and that you can talk to Him at any time.

10. Rejoice that you can worship in the company of many of God's saints.

Accept the Services of the Church

Accept the services which the church can provide. Worship faithfully and gain strength through hearing the Word of God and through praying and praising God. Attend Holy Communion regularly to receive the blessings which come to you through this means of grace. Gratefully remember the Christian education which you have received, but at the same time remember that you must never stop growing and learning as a Christian. For that reason attend Bible classes faithfully and regularly and participate to the fullest extent. It is impossible to remain a Christian without using the Word of God, and the Bible class offers a fine opportunity for such use. Dwight L. Moody said: "A man can no more take in a supply of grace for the future than he can eat enough for the next six months or take sufficient air into his lungs at once to sustain life for a week to come. We must draw upon God's boundless stores of grace from day to day as we need it." You need God's Word as you need your daily food.

There are other services of the church which you will find useful and stimulating. The organizations of the church for young people and adults can provide instruction, fellowship, and Christian recreation for you, no matter what your age may be. Participate in their activities. Use the services of your pastor and teachers. They do not forget you as soon as you have finished school, or the Senior Department of your Sunday school, or your confirmation instruction. Their advice and guidance is yours for the asking. Honor and respect them for what they have done for you, and look to them as spiritual advisers whom you can trust. They are at your service.

Give Your Services to the Church

But keep in mind that the church is not there only to serve you. The church needs you. Building God's kingdom is every Christian's duty and privilege, yours also. Pray and give generously of your money that God's Word may be preached and taught in churches and in church schools everywhere. But prayer and the giving of money can never take the place of bearing personal witness to Christ. Speak to people of their Savior yourself. Show them by a Christian life what Christ has done for you and what He can do for them if they believe and accept Him. You are to be a missionary. "Preach the Gospel" was said by Jesus to you. You cannot escape the duty and do not want to miss the privilege. The sooner you start to witness, the sooner you will live the full life of the Christian.

There are other ways in which you can serve the church. Very likely your church has a young people's organization. Join it, and take part in its activities. Work for it, and don't sit on the sidelines or criticize. The way to learn to love a cause is to work for it. You may be able to sing in the choir. In the course of time you may be able to teach Sunday school. You are part of the congregation, and its work is your work. When once you get that spirit, you will have come close to understanding what God meant when He said that you are a priest of God and that you are a "fellow citizen with the saints and a member of the household of God" (Eph. 2:19). You will find new opportunities for service as time goes on.

Church Membership Calls for Action

In thinking of yourself as a church member, you need to keep in mind that your membership is not a lazy belonging to a congregation where you receive all the blessings, but where you don't have to do anything. You would not want to live that way. Christian church membership calls for action on your part. With every privilege goes a responsibility. The great joy and privilege of church membership is in knowing that you are Christ's own through faith; but the joy and responsibility of serving Christ as a grateful believer is just as great. "Serve the Lord with gladness!" (Ps. 100:2)

Prayer

Holy triune God, Father, Son, and Holy Spirit, I confess that I am unworthy of Your grace and the privilege of worship. Forgive my lukewarmness and my neglect. Help me to love You more and to worship You with a believing and thankful heart. Make me diligent in hearing and in studying Your Word. Bless Christian pastors and teachers everywhere, and open the hearts of all people to the message of Your Word. Make me a willing worker in Your kingdom, and show me how I can participate in Your work. Help me to proclaim Your wonderful love that more and more people may come to repentance and faith and to eternal life. Hear me, Lord, for the sake of Jesus Christ, my Savior. Amen.

VI. LIVING FOR CHRIST WHEREVER YOU ARE

You Are to Be a Salt and a Light

When you made your confirmation vow to be on God's side and not the devil's, you promised that you would live for Christ wherever you are, difficult as it might be. You promised that with God's help you would be "the salt of the earth" and "the light of the world." You will want to reread what God says about that in Matt. 5:13-16: "You are the salt of the earth. But if the salt has lost its taste, how shall its saltness be restored? It is no longer good for anything except to be thrown out and trodden under foot by men.

You are the light of the world. A city set on a hill cannot be hid. Nor do men light a lamp and put it under a bushel, but on a stand, and it gives light to all in the house. Let your light so shine before men that they may see your good works and give glory to your Father who is in heaven."

Jesus sets a high standard here. As salt gives taste and flavor to the food which you eat and keeps it from spoiling, so you are to be a wholesome salt in a wicked world. As a lamp lights up the darkness, so you are to be a light in a sinful world. You are to stand out as a Christian. You are to be different from the people of the world. It is a pity that many Christians are much like the people of the world. If you go into their houses, you can scarcely tell the difference. The pictures and the magazines are like those of the people of the world. When you hear them talk, they often use the same foul language, and they curse like the people of the world. You find some of them with the world in the same places of entertainment, even though the entertainment may be sinful; you find them dishonest in business; and often on Sunday mornings you find them in bed instead of in church. That is all wrong. Wherever the Christian goes, he should live so that Christ is glorified in his life. That is what God expects of you, and that is what you promised.

Choose the Right Kind of Friends

You will have to be careful about many things if you want to live your life for Christ. For one thing, you will have to be careful in the choice of your friends. Our friends have a great influence on us. We want to do what they do and go to the places where they go. Even if deep down in our hearts we really don't want to, we are afraid to offend our friends, and we often do what they do and go with them where they go, even if we know that it is wrong. You are known by the company you keep. Many a Christian boy and girl was lost eternally because of the wrong choice of friends. Avoid bad company.

If you pray and think a while, you will be able to see what kind of friends you ought to choose. Certainly they ought to be people whom you can hope to meet in heaven. Certainly you will want friends who can inspire you to think noble and God-pleasing thoughts and who can encourage you to do what is right. You want friends who can pull you up, not down; friends who are a strength to you when weakness and temptations come; who can give you Christian comfort in sorrow; who will stand by you in trouble; unselfish, kind, helpful Christian friends. That is the kind of friend you want to be, and that is the kind of friends you want to choose. Then you will be in safe company, and your parents can have trust and confidence in you. You will at the same time be in the kind of company where you will likely find a Christian husband or wife in the course of time. Friends are important. We should choose friends that love Christ as we do. Above all, make Christ your dearest Friend. He gave His life purely out of love for you.

When You Meet Unbelievers

You are to be a salt and a light also among the unbelievers. You will meet unbelievers and sometimes scoffers at your work and elsewhere. Here is a story which shows wrong action in the company of unbelievers: A young man decided to go away to work in a lumber camp. His friends warned him that he would have trouble. The lumberjacks in that particular camp were rough characters, and they would ridicule him for his religion and perhaps even persecute him for it. But the young man went, saying he was sure he would get along all right. After some months he returned, hale and hearty, and his friends asked him how he had gotten along. Were the lumberjacks really as rough as they had been pictured? Did they curse and swear and gamble and scoff and blaspheme as it had been said? The young man said that they were fully as bad as they had been described, but that he got along with them very well. "How did you do it?" the friends asked. "Oh, that was easy," the young man said. "They never found out that I was a Christian."

This young man hid his light under a bushel, and he had failed miserably in his duty. If he was a Christian at all, he was a weakling and a coward, for he should have witnessed to his Savior and borne the ridicule.

When you meet with unbelievers, you are not to be ashamed of your Christianity or afraid to confess it. You are to testify, because only so can unbelievers learn to know about their Savior and His love. "Let your light so shine before men that they may see your good works and give glory to your Father who is in heaven."

Overcoming Sin

One of your daily trials will be sin. You will be living with sin all the time. It is a sad fact that even the most sincere Christian sins. That does not make sin any less serious, for sin separates from God. When you have sinned, the devil will tell you that there is no use in trying to follow God, that you will fail every time. To discourage you, he will remind you of your many failures. Do not listen to the devil. Because of your sin, Christ died for you. As surely as you sin daily, so surely God forgives daily. Do not be like Cain or Judas, who despaired of God's mercy and doubted His ability and willingness to forgive. You know what happened to both of them. When you have sinned, think of the Prodigal Son, who returned humbly and penitently to his father. Think of the Publican, who said, "God be merciful to me, a sinner"; or of Zacchaeus, who repented and loved and served Jesus from then on.

God is ready to forgive even your most shameful sins, and this fact should lead you to true repentance: Sincere sorrow for your sin, faith in Jesus as your Savior, and the desire and determination to avoid sin in the future. "Though your sins are like scarlet, they shall be as white as snow; though they are red like crimson, they shall become like wool" (Is. 1:18). But do not make God's mercy an excuse for continuing in sin, for God also says:

"Wash yourselves, make yourselves clean; put away the evil of your doings from before My eyes; cease to do evil; learn to do good" (Is. 1:16-17). In other words, confess your sins daily and accept the divine forgiveness, and also daily make up your mind to serve your Lord and Savior wholeheartedly. The battle will be renewed every day, and every day you will be victorious until the great day comes when you will be delivered from all your sins and temptations, when you will be with Jesus in heaven forever. That day is worth waiting and praying for.

Living for Christ in Trouble

You are also to live for Christ when troubles come. There will be troubles in your life — sickness, sorrow, death of a loved one, poverty, or whatever it may be. Not all people have the same troubles, but all have troubles, some more and some less. It is hard to live for Christ in trouble. When serious troubles come to us, we may want to say: "Why did this have to happen to me?" "What did I do to deserve this?" You may have heard Christian people say this, but it is not the way a Christian should look at trouble. The Christian knows that troubles will come and that God sends them for his good.

It is easy to be a fair-weather Christian. When everything goes well, when we have everything we want, when there is no pain or sorrow, it is easy to say, "God is good." But the fair-weather Christian cannot stand up under the trials of life. When troubles strike him, he will complain and doubt God's goodness. Many have cast their faith overboard because they did not believe that God was fair to them when He sent troubles for their good. Fair-weather Christianity is like a frail flower that may be ever so beautiful for a time, but when the frost comes, it fades and dies. Real Christianity is like the countless perennial flowers that stand up through storm and sunshine, through summer and winter, and each spring come out as beautiful as ever.

You know that troubles are due to sin. You have observed how the deadwood and harmful growth are pruned out of rosebushes, grapevines, or trees. At the time it may seem as if the pruner is too ruthless with his shears and saw, but he knows what is best, and the flourishing of the plants soon proves the rightness of his action. So you may well think of troubles as a pruning which God uses to clip our pride, to show us the foolishness of attaching our hearts to earthly things, to remind us of our weakness and frailty, and to draw us closer to Himself. Worrying and complaining about troubles is therefore foolish and sinful. Rather, you are to see God's hand also in your troubles, submit yourself to His direction and will, and trust that "all things work together for good to them that love God" (Rom. 8:28). You will still pray daily and fervently for deliverance, but at the same time you are willing to accept God's own answer to your prayers, even if His answer is not exactly what you had wished.

You should always remember that life on earth is a preparation for heaven and that your faith can make even this life on earth a forecourt of heaven in spite of its troubles. Even when trials continue long, you know that they will end in time and that you will one day stand in the presence of God and His angels where there will be only joy. Surrender yourself to God completely, live your life for God and your fellowmen, and be prepared to suffer and to die when your last hour comes. God will help you say: "The sufferings of this present time are not worth comparing with the glory that is to be revealed in us." (Rom. 8:18)

You can, therefore, live joyfully from day to day, no matter what the conditions of your life may be. When the apostle Paul said to the Philippians (4:4), "Rejoice in the Lord always; again I will say, Rejoice," he knew very well that they had troubles and would have more troubles. Yet he said they should always rejoice, even in trouble. Living in God's grace with all our sins forgiven is so great a blessing that our joy breaks through even in time of sorrow, as you have seen the bright sun break through the darkest clouds. The life of the Christian is a joyful, victorious life because God forgives his sins and supplies all his other needs.

Living for Christ in Everything

Whether it is work or play, pleasure or sorrow, you as a Christian will want to live for Christ. You will serve Christ in serving your fellowmen. It is as if Christ were saying to you: "I have no hands but your hands; you must do My work for Me and serve your fellowmen. I have no feet but your feet; you must go where there is need for help. I have no mouth but your mouth; you must preach My Word for Me." That is how closely you are tied up with Christ and His work. His work is your work. His pleasure is your pleasure. His will is your will. That is the Christian way.

You can dream to your heart's content of doing great things for your Savior, for your fellowmen, for your country, for your parents, for your friends, and then go out and do them. In that way you will play the part you are supposed to play as a Christian. Your love for Christ will enable you to live victoriously and joyfully for Him. Say, "Lord, may Your will be done," and then meet every situation with confidence in God and with your chest out.

Go All Out for Christ

You will do great things for Christ if you believe with all your heart that He is your Savior and if you are grateful for His love. Let love rule your life, love for God and love for men. If you love people, you will think of others first, and you will be a good servant of your Lord and Savior. Be tolerant and respect the rights and ideas of others, unless they are contrary to the Word of God. Find ways to serve others. Respect and obey authority, the authority of God, of your parents, and of your government, and you will be happy. Practice kind dealings and good manners in everything. Work hard at your job, and in everything remember that you are working for the Lord and not yourself. Your time, your abilities, your possessions — they all belong to God, and you must use them according to His pleasure. Go all out for Christ. Then you will be a good steward to whom the Lord Jesus will one day say: "Well done, good and faithful servant. You have been faithful over a little, I will set you over much; enter into the joy of your Master." (Matt. 25:21)

That will be the day when you will forget entirely about the sorrows and difficulties that you have had, and you will ever after live in the presence of the Lord, the angels, and all the saints in heaven.

Prayer

Merciful God, thank You for having made me a Christian. Forgive the many times that I have been a fair-weather Christian. Fill my heart with love and zeal for You, keep my faith strong, and help me always to glorify

You. Make me a salt and a light in the world. Give me friends that will be a strength and encouragement to me; help me to overcome trials and temptations; forgive my many sins, and make me willing to forgive those who have sinned against me. Help me to speak Your Word when it is easy and when it is hard. Your love has been wonderful to me; help me to love You and the people around me. In Your own good time take me to heaven; in Jesus' name. Amen.